MARVEL

GUARDIANS OF THE GALAXY

ROCKET'S GUIDE
A FUR-FLYIN' LOOK AT INTERSTELLAR HEROES AND SCUM

BY MARC SUMERAK

becker&mayer!
BOOK PRODUCERS

TABLE OF CONTENTS

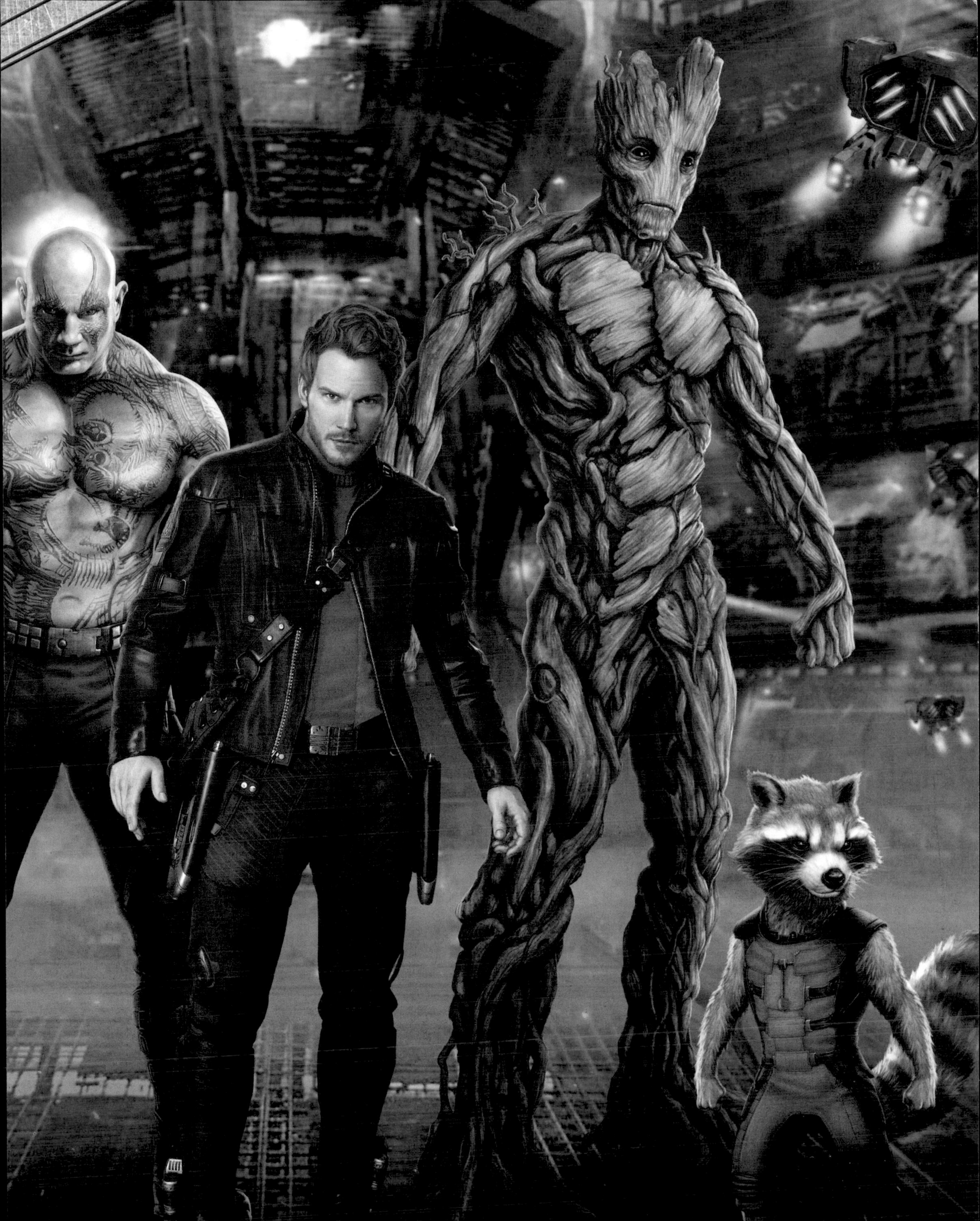

INTRODUCTION

Hey there, you hairless weirdos! It's me, your old pal Rocket.

If you're reading this, you're probably hoping to get the inside scoop on what made me one of the galaxy's most in-demand bounty hunters. And who am I to deny my adoring public the details they so desperately desire?

I've been kinda busy doing the hero thing lately, so I thought I might as well pass my wisdom along to the next generation—and make a couple bucks doing it!

In these pages, you'll get to meet some of the hottest tickets in the known universe. Heroes, villains, it don't matter, right? They're all paychecks to an aspiring bounty hunter like you!

Capture just one of these guys, and you'll be living large. Screw it up, and you'll find yourself on the wrong end of a necroblaster—or worse!

As a bonus, I'll also include some info on their signature vehicles and favorite hideouts, to give you a leg up when you're tracking them down.

But remember, I am in no way suggesting you should take on Thanos alone. I'm just passing you the knowledge. What you do with it is up to you.

Good luck. You're gonna need it . . .

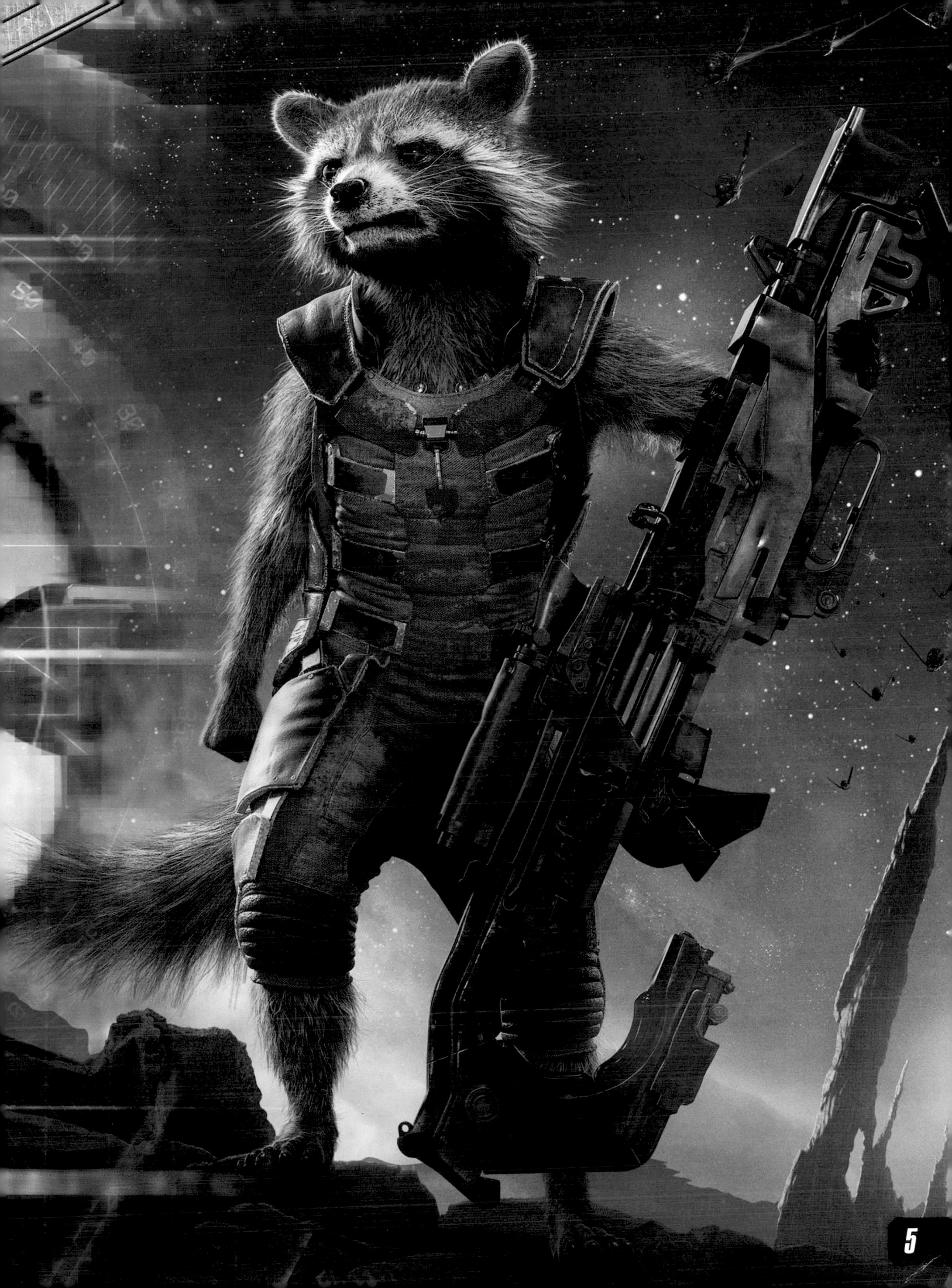

STAR-LORD
(aka PETER QUILL)

Trust me, this guy is more interesting than he looks.

Star-Lord may have gotten his boring human face and his obsession with Earth culture from his mom, but his dad is actually some super-powerful unidentified alien being. I know, right?

When he was a kid, Quill was abducted by space pirates called Ravagers (I'll get to those jerks later). They taught him everything he knows about cheating and stealing, shaping him into a self-proclaimed "legendary outlaw."

He's got a decent ship. He's a good fighter (and a terrible dancer). And he just doesn't know how to give up . . . even when he probably should.

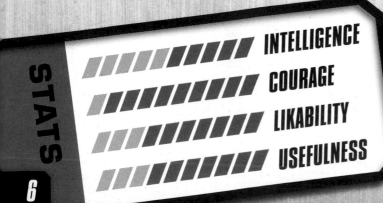

INTELLIGENCE

COURAGE

LIKABILITY

USEFULNESS

MAIN WEAPON

Double-barreled quad blasters. The top barrel shoots fire, the bottom barrel shoots electricity. Quad means "four," but Quill was never too great at math. There's also that ancient music-playing relic of his. That thing'll give you a headache that won't quit.

TARGET

WANTED: Star-Lord

BOUNTY: I'm not saying I'd turn him in, but if I did? I know I could get at least 40,000 units. (I'd totally turn him in.)

ROCKET'S RECAP
Somewhere between fearless and clueless.

GROOT

Whether I'm hunting for bounty or breaking out of prison, there's no one I'd rather have by my side than my old pal, Groot.

You may recognize him as the galaxy's favorite walking, talking giant tree, but technically he's a Flora Colossus from Planet X. That means he can grow fast, hit hard, and regenerate his body from even the smallest splinter.

Groot is a plant of few words. Only three actually. "I AM GROOT." That's it. But what he lacks in vocabulary, he makes up in courage and loyalty. I couldn't imagine an adventure without him.

INTELLIGENCE

COURAGE

LIKABILITY

USEFULNESS

MAIN WEAPON

His limbs. They say a tree is only as strong as his branches, and Groot's are as strong as they come. He can extend them into long, flexible vines that he can tangle around his enemies. Or he can just use them to whack people unconscious. Either way works.

TARGET

WANTED: Groot

BOUNTY: Wouldn't trade this guy for a billion units. Two billion, though . . .

ROCKET'S RECAP
Body of wood, heart of gold.

DRAX

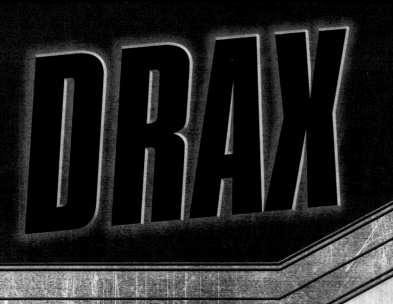

Me and Drax didn't exactly see eye-to-eye at first. Partly because he's so much taller than me, but mostly because we hated each other's guts. Turns out, we make a pretty good team.

After his family was nixed by Ronan, Drax began a brutal quest for revenge that earned him the nickname "The Destroyer." Which has a way better ring to it than "The Kree Puncher."

Drax comes from a species that doesn't understand symbols or metaphors, so regular conversations can be a bit of a chore. Fortunately, what we do best doesn't require a whole lot of talking!

INTELLIGENCE

COURAGE

LIKABILITY

USEFULNESS

MAIN WEAPON

Knives. Drax carries a pair of these razor-sharp bad boys to slice and dice his way through armies of foes. Though his knife skills would put the universe's best chefs to shame, Drax is also just as comfortable using his bare fists to tenderize his opponents.

TARGET

WANTED: Drax

BOUNTY: I know a few Kree who would pay at least 300,000 units for Drax, dead or alive. Good luck with that!

ROCKET'S RECAP

Mean green fighting machine!

GAMORA

In a universe as big as ours, it takes a lot to build a solid reputation. I should know. So the fact that the assassin named Gamora is feared by so many people on so many worlds says it all.

After Thanos offed her parents, the creep raised Gamora as his own daughter. He shaped her into the perfect fighting machine, upgrading her body with all sorts of cybernetic enhancements.

But there was one thing that Thanos couldn't replace: her soul. Turns out, she still had a good one hiding in there.

INTELLIGENCE

COURAGE

LIKABILITY

USEFULNESS

MAIN WEAPON

Retractable blade. Gamora's favorite sword can cut through almost anything or anyone. Just ask poor Groot. When not in use, the blade folds into its hilt. A small throwing dagger can be detached from the sword and hurled with deadly accuracy, so look out!

TARGET

WANTED: Gamora

BOUNTY: Last I checked, Gamora had a bounty of 50 million units on her head. I'd rather keep my own.

ROCKET'S RECAP
Deadliest woman in the galaxy.

ROCKET

Then there's me, the beloved intergalactic sensation known as Rocket. One hundred sixty-eight grets of pure awesome.

I don't like to talk about my past much. Let's just say the scientists on Halfworld did some horrifically illegal experiments to turn me into the wise-cracking, gun-toting, butt-kicking Rocket you know and love. I didn't ask to get made, but I might as well make the best of it while I'm here, right? My lifespan ain't that long anyway.

Never thought I'd find myself guarding the galaxy, but this whole "hero" thing feels kinda good.

STATS

///////// INTELLIGENCE

///////// COURAGE

///////// LIKABILITY

///////// USEFULNESS

MAIN WEAPON

The Hadron Enforcer. I built this baby myself out of parts I salvaged from Quill's ship. It's capable of unleashing a particle blast that could shatter a moon. While all guns may look comically oversized in my hands, this one actually has the power to match!

TARGET

WANTED: Rocket
BOUNTY: Whatever you got, it ain't enough.

ROCKET'S RECAP

Fierce, furry, and fantastic!

THE MILANO

What do you get when you take a beat up Ravager M-Ship and fill it with worthless Earth memorabilia and five world-class heroes? You get our current mobile base of operations, Star-Lord's personal starship, *The Milano*.

Quill treats this thing like his baby. His filthy, barely-functioning baby. When *The Milano* got trashed fighting Ronan, I swear Quill started to cry.

Good thing the Nova Corps salvaged the ship's parts and rebuilt it, better than new.

Bad thing that they salvaged that stupid tape deck. After hearing the same songs a billion times, the only feeling I'm "hooked on" is pure rage.

An M-Ship can fit a few crew members pretty comfortably, but if you live in one together for long periods of time, it starts to get a bit cramped. Trust me.

Sure, there are plenty of better-looking ships out there, but I'll admit, this one's got solid speed, good maneuverability, and a whole lot of firepower. Now, if only Quill would let a real pilot behind the controls . . .

M-SHIPS

Like I said, *The Milano* may have a fancy name, but it's really just tricked out Ravager M-Ship. M-Ships are the personal spacecraft that the Ravagers take on scouting missions and raids.

If I could convince Yondu to give me my own M-Ship—or if I could distract him for long enough—I'd definitely take one.

YONDU
AND THE RAVAGERS

Remember those space pirates who abducted Quill when he was a kid? Those were the Ravagers—a motley assortment of thieves, outlaws, and mercenaries roaming space in search of their next big score.

The Ravagers are willing to steal anything from anybody. Even each other. To be honest, I probably would have fit in pretty well with them . . . if they all didn't smell so bad!

The captain of the Ravagers, Yondu Udonta, likes to think he's the meanest scoundrel on the space ways, but he's really a big softy deep down. After all, he kept his crew from killing Quill for 26 years. He must be a saint . . . or an idiot!

INTELLIGENCE

COURAGE

LIKABILITY

USEFULNESS

MAIN WEAPON

Yaka Arrow. This sharp metal projectile is controlled through a series of high-pitched (and extremely annoying) whistles. Yondu has mastered this crazy thing and is quick to turn it against anyone who betrays him. If you ever hear him whistling a tune, no matter how happy, run!

TARGET

WANTED: Yondu Udonta

BOUNTY: Yondu could fetch you 500,000 units or more. Most of the other Ravagers aren't worth their weight in scrap.

ROCKET'S RECAP
The bad, the worse, and the really ugly.

THE ECLECTOR

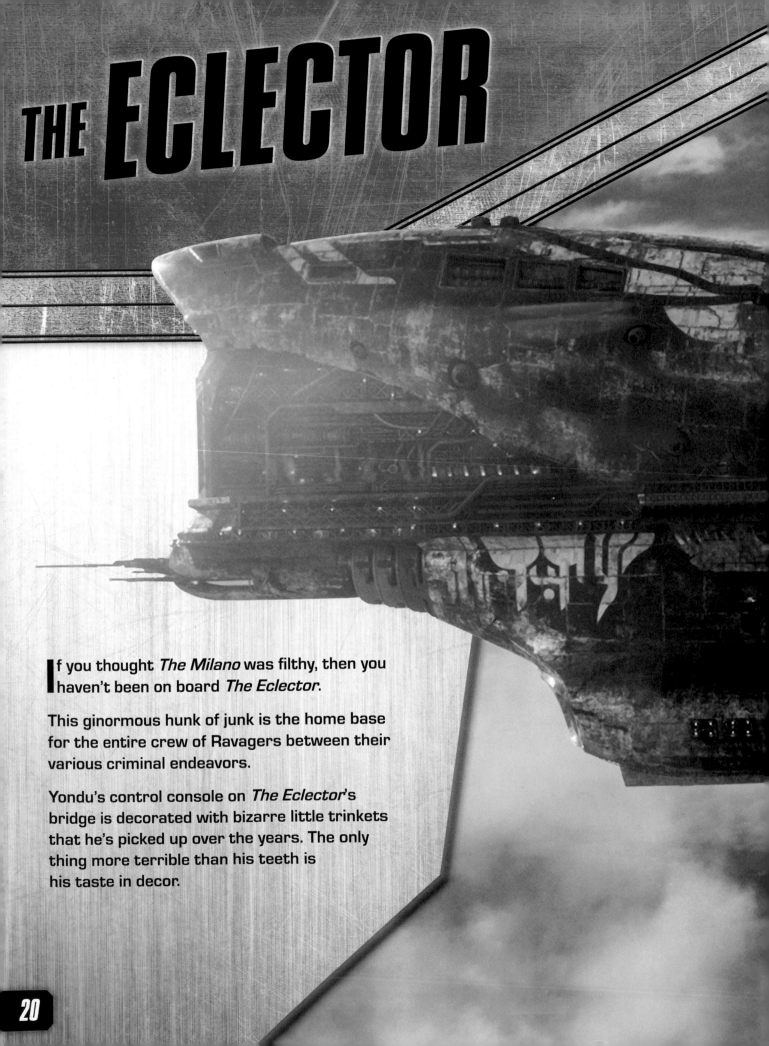

If you thought *The Milano* was filthy, then you haven't been on board *The Eclector*.

This ginormous hunk of junk is the home base for the entire crew of Ravagers between their various criminal endeavors.

Yondu's control console on *The Eclector*'s bridge is decorated with bizarre little trinkets that he's picked up over the years. The only thing more terrible than his teeth is his taste in decor.

Quill grew up on this flying trash heap, so he knows what's hiding behind every rusty door. From what he's told me, you should probably just avoid opening any of them if you value your health or your sanity.

The Ravagers are already notorious for being the filthiest, nastiest pirates on the space ways, so it's only appropriate that their ship should follow that theme. But seriously, to get a ship this dirty takes work. It's almost like Yondu pays his men extra to NOT do their chores.

THE NOVA CORPS

The Nova Corps is basically an intergalactic police force. And for a long time, I was one of their most frequent customers.

On their home planet Xandar, the Nova Corps are quick to arrest anyone who commits a crime, no matter how small. They also run a bunch of maximum-security prisons floating throughout the galaxy . . . though they haven't built one that can keep me in yet!

Most Nova Corpsmen are by-the-books do-gooders with no sense of adventure. A couple of them are okay, though, like my pal Rhomann Dey. He knows that to save the world, sometimes you gotta break a few laws.

STATS

INTELLIGENCE

COURAGE

LIKABILITY

USEFULNESS

MAIN WEAPON

Wrist cannon. The members of the Nova Corps have a double-barreled laser cannon mounted to the gauntlet on their right arms. It may not look like much, but it can take down a guy three times my size with one well-placed shot. Also, it'll burn the fur right off your tail.

TARGET

WANTED: Rhomann Dey

BOUNTY: Most Nova Corpsmen are a dime a dozen. This guy's worth at least twice that.

ROCKET'S RECAP
So good it makes me queasy.

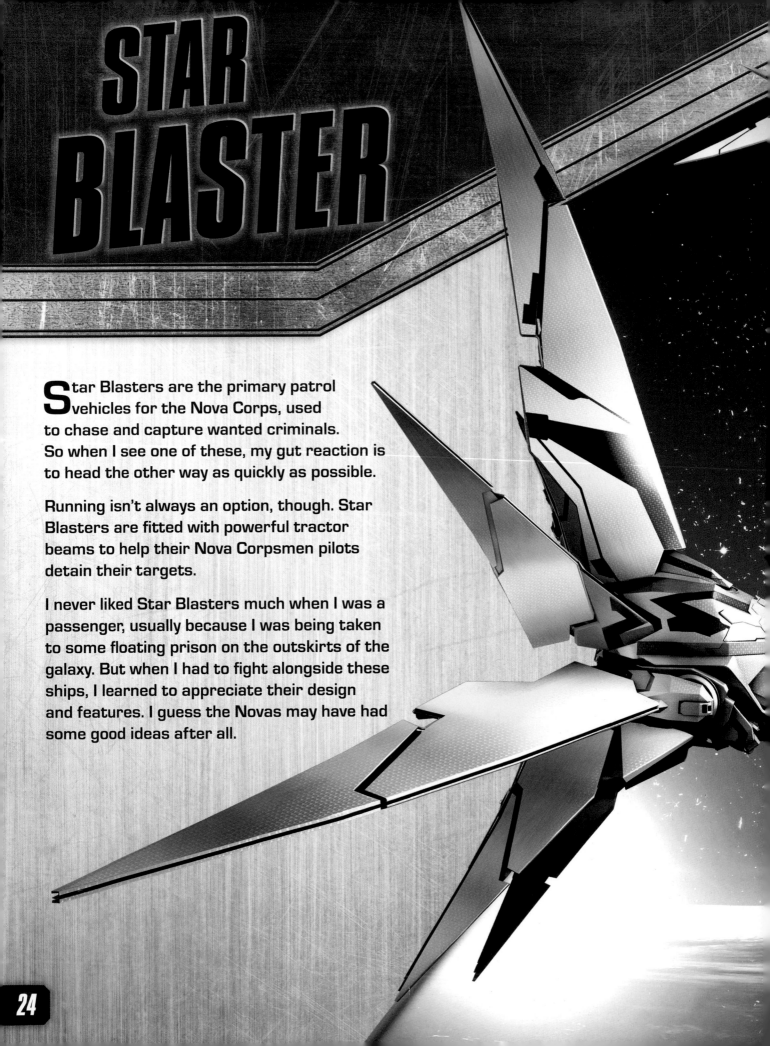

STAR BLASTER

Star Blasters are the primary patrol vehicles for the Nova Corps, used to chase and capture wanted criminals. So when I see one of these, my gut reaction is to head the other way as quickly as possible.

Running isn't always an option, though. Star Blasters are fitted with powerful tractor beams to help their Nova Corpsmen pilots detain their targets.

I never liked Star Blasters much when I was a passenger, usually because I was being taken to some floating prison on the outskirts of the galaxy. But when I had to fight alongside these ships, I learned to appreciate their design and features. I guess the Novas may have had some good ideas after all.

One of the Star Blasters' coolest features is their ability to link together via energy fields and form a nearly impenetrable blockade. Link a few ships to stop a wild chase, or link hundreds to protect entire planets!

If things get too rowdy, the ships also have powerful offensive laser cannons. Most Nova Corpsmen try to keep the peace without them, but some are just itching for an excuse to pull the trigger.

XANDAR

I've got mixed feelings about Xandar.

It's a bit too clean. The people are a bit too nice. Its three suns are a bit too bright. And the Nova Corps are a bit too eager to lock me in a cell. The place is just not my speed.

I should've left Xandar far behind me when I had the chance, but instead I came back and helped save it from total annihilation. I'm a bit of an enigma that way.

Truth is, despite its shiny exterior, Xandar has seen its fair share of hard times. The Xandarians and the Kree waged war for over a thousand years. While a peace treaty was signed, Kree terrorists like Ronan refused to honor it, making Xandar a target for all sorts of attacks.

Unlike the Kree extremists, the Xandarians managed to rise above the hostility. They built a society where diversity, culture, and peace flourish. That took hard work, and I can respect it. As much as I hate to admit it, a big portion of the credit goes to the Nova Corps. Xandar is their headquarters and the capital of the Nova Empire.

NOVA PRIME

Despite what some so-called heroes may think, you can't just rush into an epic battle with only part of a plan. Luckily, there ain't no better strategist than Irani Rael, also known as Nova Prime. She's got a commanding presence that has earned her the respect of her Nova Corpsmen—and even yours truly!

Of course, now that I fought to save their planet, the Xandarians kinda love me. Maybe it's time to go back and take another look around. I am a hero there, after all. If that doesn't get me free stuff . . . well, I'll probably just steal it anyway. Can't expect to keep my record clean forever!

THE KYLN

Looking to get away from the hustle and bustle of everyday life? Have I got the vacation spot for you! Just go to Xandar, commit a minor offense—you know, like kidnapping or arson—and you'll be whisked away on an all-expenses-paid, one-way trip to the galaxy's most luxurious maximum security prison satellite: The Kyln!

Wait . . . did I say "luxurious"? I think I meant the opposite of that.

I've broken out of dozens of prisons in my day, yet somehow this one still holds my fondest memories . . .

Welcome to general population, where the meanest of the mean are waiting for someone new to be the target for their misguided aggression. Remember that guy who you cheated out of 50,000 units in those illegal Orloni fights? He's here, too . . . and he's so excited to have you as his new bunkmate! Good times!

But that ain't to say the place is all bad. We did some time there, and even though the accommodations were one-star at best, it's the first place where we got to take a break from trying to kill each other and really bonded as a team.

In the Kyln, it's all about who you know. Make the right connections—and steal the right tech—and you'll be able to break out of there before lights out. Make the wrong connections, though, and you won't even make it to lunch. Heck, you'll probably BE lunch.

KNOWHERE

I know what you're about to ask. "Is that a giant floating head on the edge of space?" Probably followed immediately by, "Why are we going inside of that giant floating head on the edge of space?!?"

Because it's the coolest place in the galaxy, that's why. So stop your nagging and enjoy the ride.

Welcome to Knowhere. Called that because:

A) it's on the edge of nowhere;

B) there's nowhere else like it;

C) and there ain't nowhere else I'd like to spend my days off.

Quill says the "K" makes it a pun. I don't get it.

Built inside the decapitated head of some ancient cosmic being called a Celestial, Knowhere started off as a mining colony. Turns out, all the gunk inside of this poor guy's enormous noggin—the bone, brains, and various juices—is worth a fortune on the black market, so the Tivan Group laid claim and started mining.

THE COLLECTOR

The Tivan Group was named after its eccentric founder, Tanaleer Tivan. They call this freak The Collector because he keeps an entire museum full of the universe's most bizarre creatures and artifacts right in the center of Knowhere. (As if the place wasn't already weird enough.)

The Collector is willing to pay just about any price to get his hands on cool new things. He even offered to buy Groot once. If it's extremely rare or insanely powerful, he's gotta have it.

One time, he almost paid us four billion units for a stupid orb that Quill recovered on Morag! It didn't work out. I don't want to talk about it.

If you're looking for a decent meal and a bit of illicit gambling, head to the Boot of Jemiah and tell 'em that Groot sent you. Don't mention me, though. I still haven't paid my tab from my last visit.

THE SAKAARANS

Looking for a bunch of mindless drones to fight your battles for you? Look no further than the Sakaarans. This race of gross insectoid aliens apparently has nothing better to do than to wage other people's wars.

Ronan relied on the Sakaarans for combat support, treating them as completely disposable soldiers in the war against Xandar. The Sakaarans excel as fighters and pilots, but completely lack any social skills. Good thing they're fun to shoot.

Drax calls Sakaarans "paper people," probably because of how they just crumple up when he hits 'em.

STATS

/////////////	INTELLIGENCE
/////////////	COURAGE
/////////////	LIKABILITY
/////////////	USEFULNESS

MAIN WEAPON

Necroblasters. These energy rifles are the standard issue weapon for Sakaaran troops. "Necro" means death, so that should be a pretty solid warning that you should avoid getting hit by one. The Sakaarans have also built larger cannons that use an amplified necroblast to take down starships.

TARGET

WANTED: The Sakaarans

BOUNTY: If I got a single unit for every one of these goons I took down, I'd be rich!

ROCKET'S RECAP

Free target practice.

KORATH
THE PURSUER

Korath is a Kree mercenary serving under the command of Ronan. He first crossed paths with Quill on the planet Morag, where they were both looking for the same ancient artifact. He's been a thorn in our sides ever since.

He is an expert fighter and marksman, and his skills are augmented by a series of cybernetic implants that enhance his agility, durability, and strength to Drax-like levels. Korath is often seen leading troops of Sakaaran soldiers into battle.

Also, based on his name, I guess he's also pretty good at pursuing things.

120   110   100

STATS

///////// INTELLIGENCE
///////// COURAGE
///////// LIKABILITY
///////// USEFULNESS

MAIN WEAPON

Really big gun. Korath is sorta like me in one way: he enjoys the firepower of a weapon much larger than he actually needs. He could probably kill you with a toothpick and a rubber band, but it looks so much cooler when he does it with a huge bolt of super-charged plasma!

TARGET

WANTED: Korath the Pursuer

BOUNTY: The Nova Corps has a reward of 30 million units for Korath's capture. Not too shabby.

ROCKET'S RECAP
A Target Worth Pursuing.

RONAN
THE ACCUSER

This guy. Not one of my favorites.

Ronan lives to punish his enemies. He's all about destroying the Xandarians, whom he blames for thousands of years of war and death. He was even willing to team up with Thanos to make it happen. He's a Kree, so he's super strong, super durable, and super annoying.

If it wasn't for his psychotic rage and unquenchable thirst for power, Ronan might be all right. Then again, without all that rage, Ronan just wouldn't be Ronan.

I think I could live with that.

////// INTELLIGENCE

////// COURAGE

////// LIKABILITY

////// USEFULNESS

MAIN WEAPON

The Universal Weapon. (I didn't name it. That's really what it's called.) It looks like a hammer thing on a pole, and besides smashing heads, it shoots out a blast of force that can practically take you apart. You don't want to know what happens when it is attached to an Infinity Stone . . .

TARGET

WANTED: Ronan the Accuser

BOUNTY: Somewhere around a zillion units?

ROCKET'S RECAP
The Walking Tantrum.

THE DARK ASTER

This monstrosity is Ronan's warship, *The Dark Aster*. It's a flying fortress of doom.

Despite its foreboding appearance, the ship's security isn't that great. If you can blow a hole in the starboard hull, disable a power core or two, and get onto the ship's flight deck, you've got yourself a brand new ship of death!

Of course, the ship also houses hordes of Sakaaran soldiers ready to lay down their miserable lives to protect their big boss. Oh, and did I mention that they each have their own ships, too?

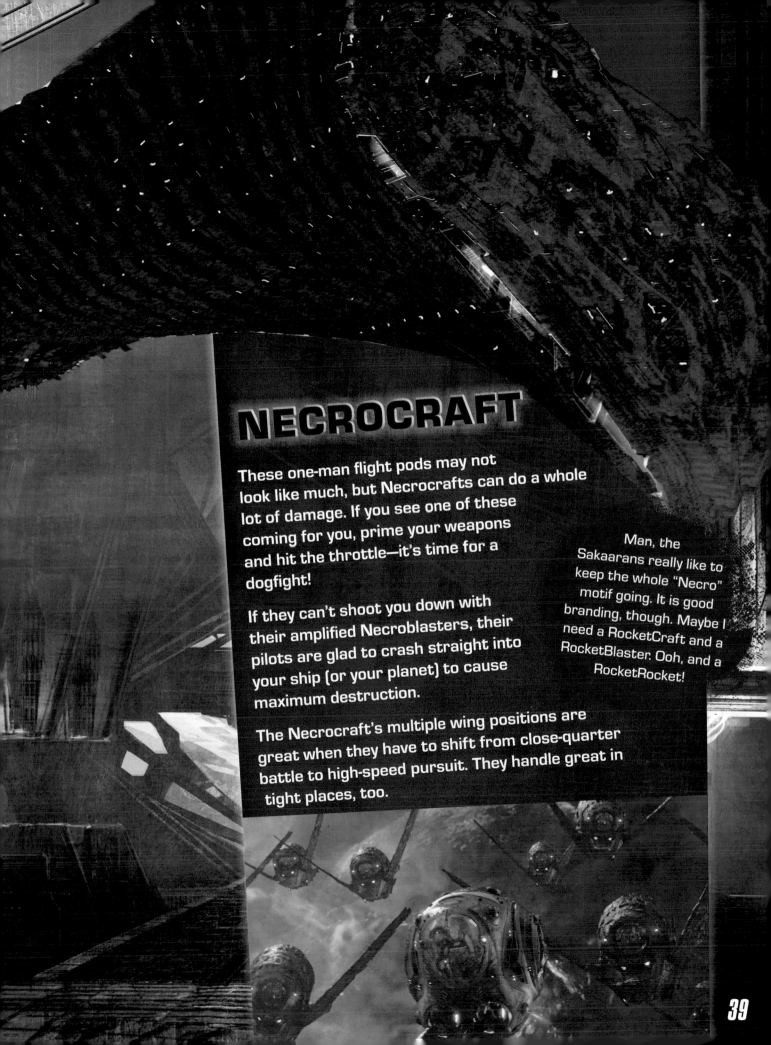

NECROCRAFT

These one-man flight pods may not look like much, but Necrocrafts can do a whole lot of damage. If you see one of these coming for you, prime your weapons and hit the throttle—it's time for a dogfight!

If they can't shoot you down with their amplified Necroblasters, their pilots are glad to crash straight into your ship (or your planet) to cause maximum destruction.

The Necrocraft's multiple wing positions are great when they have to shift from close-quarter battle to high-speed pursuit. They handle great in tight places, too.

Man, the Sakaarans really like to keep the whole "Necro" motif going. It is good branding, though. Maybe I need a RocketCraft and a RocketBlaster. Ooh, and a RocketRocket!

NEBULA

They say you can't choose your family, which is a nice way of saying that you're stuck with them, no matter how miserable they are.

Take Gamora and her adopted sister Nebula, for instance. Both were abducted by Thanos when they were young, both were modified with all sorts of high-tech nonsense, and both joined Ronan's quest to destroy Xandar.

Even though Gamora wised up and switched sides, she still says that Nebula is one of her favorite family members. Talk about dysfunctional!

STATS

||||||||||| INTELLIGENCE

||||||||||| COURAGE

||||||||| LIKABILITY

||||||||||| USEFULNESS

MAIN WEAPON

Shock batons. As if getting pummeled by a lady with cybernetic limbs wasn't enough, Nebula carries two truncheons that can release high-voltage electrical charges. And I mean the kind of high-voltage where you can see a person's whole skeleton light up from the inside of their body when they get zapped!

TARGET

WANTED: Nebula

BOUNTY: 25 million units. A step down from Gamora, but still one heck of a catch.

ROCKET'S RECAP
The Mean(er) Sister.

THANOS

Thanos is as bad as they come—a tyrant who has conquered worlds, destroyed entire species, and slaughtered his way through star systems, all while wearing a disturbing grin on his ugly purple mug.

Thanos sits on his floating throne in Sanctuary, watching as his cronies do his bidding. Those that fail him face his wrath. Those that succeed . . . well, they usually face his wrath, too.

Lately, Thanos has been on the hunt for some ultra-powerful cosmic rocks known as Infinity Stones. Not sure I want to find out what he plans to do with them!

STATS

///////// INTELLIGENCE
///////// COURAGE
///////// LIKABILITY
///////// USEFULNESS

MAIN WEAPON

Thanos doesn't need a weapon. Thanos is the weapon. He may have an army of Chitauri soldiers and strategic alliances with guys like Ronan, but when the time comes, Thanos is more than glad to take off his shiny gold gloves and beat everyone on your planet to a pulp without ever breaking a sweat.

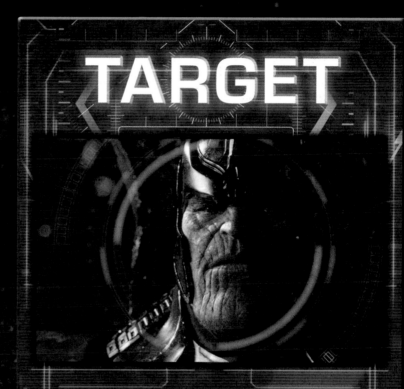

TARGET

WANTED: Thanos

BOUNTY: Billions and billions of units that you'll never collect, because once you find him, you're already dead meat.

ROCKET'S RECAP
Violet and violent.

THE ORB

Remember that ancient artifact Quill found on Morag that got everyone all up in our business? There's a reason so many people were after it. They wanted what was locked inside—an insanely powerful artifact called an Infinity Stone.

Supposedly, these stones can only be used by near-omnipotent beings (like that Celestial whose giant head is now an intergalactic rest stop).

If they're lucky, normal beings might be able to survive using an Infinity Stone for a few seconds, but only if they share the power with others. We gave it a try to save Xandar. Turns out, we were lucky. Really lucky.

After seeing what just one of these things can do, I don't think I want to be around to know what happens when all six of them get used together. But I have a bad feeling I'll be there to find out . . . because guarding the galaxy is apparently my job now.

Maybe I'll take that day off . . .

Now that Xandar is safe, the Orb has been locked away by the Nova Corps... but there are still five other Infinity Stones out there. And The Collector isn't the only weirdo who wants a full set.

AFTERWORD

There you have it, kids. Now, you've got the lowdown on the universe's hippest heroes and vilest villains. You know everything there is to know about their sweet rides and favorite hotspots. You probably know enough to make you a target for other bounty hunters.

The question is, what do you do with this inside info? Do you turn us all in, take the units, and run off to live the sweet life? Or do you use the knowledge to help us fight the good fight?

For me, it ain't even a question anymore. I may not have always been the best guy—not even close—but the people and places right here in this book have changed me for the better. Thanks to all of them, I finally know where I belong and who I'm supposed to be.

I couldn't say it any better than my best pal:

"I AM GROOT."

Can't wait to find out who you are . . .

– *Rocket*

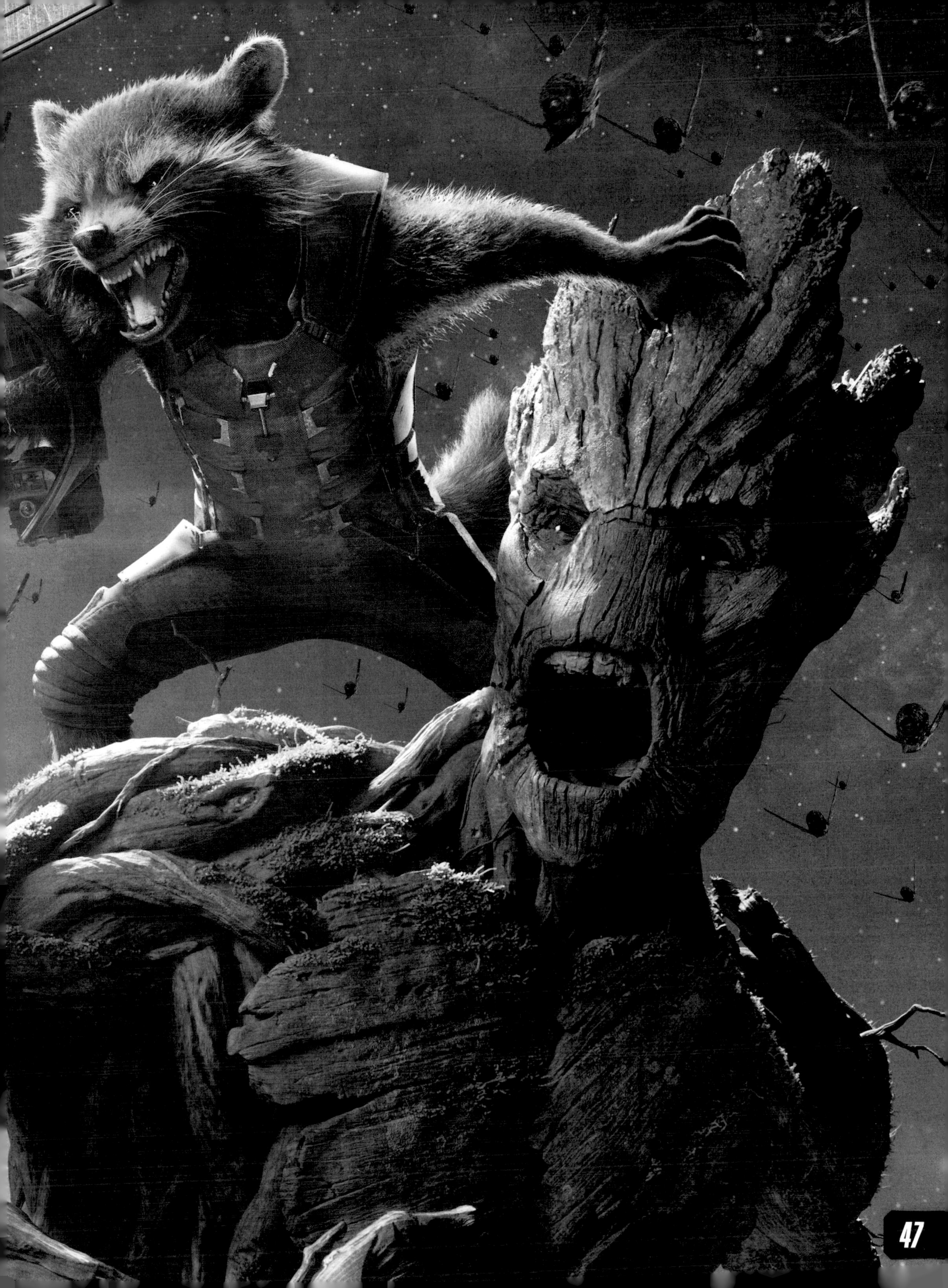

MARVEL
marvelkids.com

© 2016 MARVEL

becker&mayer!
BOOK PRODUCERS

Guardians of the Galaxy: Rocket's Guide is produced by
becker&mayer!
11120 NE 33rd Place, Suite 101
Bellevue, WA 98004
www.beckermayer.com

If you have questions or comments about this product, please visit
www.beckermayer.com/customerservice and click on Customer Service
Request Form.

Author: Marc Sumerak
Designer: Rosebud Eustace
Editor: Ashley McPhee
Production coordinator: Cindy Curren
Product sourcing: Jen Matasich

Printed in Shenzhen, China

10 9 8 7 6 5 4 3 2 1

ISBN: 978-1-60380-395-3

10/16   16251